WHAT AILETH THEE?

WHAT AILETH THEE?

THE PROBING QUESTION GOD ASKS

THAT CAN LEAD TO YOUR HEALING

REVISED EDITION

LINDA P. JONES

GLORIOUS WORKS
PUBLISHING

What Aileth Thee?

Revised Edition

By Linda P. Jones

Published by Glorious Works

Cover Design by Kainos Creative Studios Inc.

Book Design and Layout by Kainos Creative Studios Inc.

Reedited by Avodah Writing Services

For more information, contact the Publisher at gloriousworks@gmail.com.

ISBN 978-976-96300-7-9

This book is dedicated to my husband, Oliver (Guy) Jones, my Good Samaritan, who found me wounded and bleeding by the side of the road but did not pass by. Full with the unconditional love of God, he stood by my side as I confronted the pain and nursed me back to health.

Thank you, Hon. I love you.

TABLE OF CONTENTS

ACKNOWLEDGEMENTS

With gratitude to my Heavenly Father for His love that did not let me go but patiently walked me out of the wilderness of pain to drink from the wells of His Living Water.

Special thanks to the late Minister Tyrone Griffith who, after hearing me minister this word at church, encouraged me to expand it and put it in print.

Thanks to Toni Daniel who took personal interest in this work, shared some insightful thoughts with me and gave me permission to add them to this book.

Thanks to the many friends who assisted me on the road to recovery, some with their prayers and encouragement, others with their counsel and others with just a listening ear. I am indeed grateful.

FOREWORD

What Aileth Thee? takes you on a journey into the real-life drama of a rejected and abandoned single parent family, Hagar and her son Ishmael. The story of Ishmael and Hagar is usually overlooked in the context of a family in crisis. However, we learn from their experiences how God lovingly invites us to confront our pain, how He brings healing to our woundedness and then releases us into fulfilling our purpose for His glory.

In Luke 4:18-19, the first two objectives Jesus stated in His mission statement were to preach the gospel to the poor and then to heal the broken-hearted. Many of God's people who have received the message of the gospel are still broken-hearted, still in pain of some sort. The pain is either self-inflicted or as a result of someone else's indiscretion.

However, it is time for the Body of Christ to confront its pain and be healed. Time is short and the harvest of lives waiting to be reached for Christ and to be healed is plentiful.

What Aileth Thee? Christ never asks a question without having the solution or being the solution Himself.

Linda P. Jones (Rev.)

PROLOGUE

WHAT AILETH THEE?

And the LORD visited Sarah as he had said, and the LORD did unto Sarah as he had spoken. For Sarah conceived, and bare Abraham a son in his old age, at the set time of which God had spoken to him. And Abraham called the name of his son that was born unto him, whom Sarah bare to him, Isaac. And Abraham circumcised his son Isaac being eight days old, as God had commanded him. And Abraham was an hundred years old, when his son Isaac was born unto him. And Sarah said, God hath made me to laugh, so that all that hear will laugh with me. And she said, Who would have said unto Abraham, that Sarah should have given children suck? For I have born him a son in his old age.

And the child grew, and was weaned: and Abraham made a great feast the same day that Isaac was weaned. And Sarah saw the son of Hagar the Egyptian, which she had born unto Abraham, mocking. Wherefore she said unto Abraham, Cast out this bondwoman and her son: for the son of this bondwoman shall not be heir with my son, even with Isaac. And the thing was very grievous in Abraham's sight because of his son. And God said unto Abraham, Let it not be grievous in thy sight because of the lad, and because of thy bondwoman; in all that Sarah hath said unto thee, hearken unto her voice; for in Isaac shall thy seed be called. And also of the son of the bondwoman will I make a nation, because he is thy seed.

And Abraham rose up early in the morning, and took bread, and a bottle of water, and gave it unto Hagar, putting it on her shoulder, and the child, and sent her away: and she departed, and wandered in the wilderness of Beersheba. And the water was spent in the bottle, and she cast the child under one of the shrubs. And she went, and sat her down over against him a good way off, as it were a bow shot: for she said, Let me not see the death of the child. And she sat over against him, and lift up her voice, and wept. And God heard the voice of the lad; and the angel of God called to Hagar out of heaven, and said unto her, What aileth thee, Hagar? Fear not; for God hath heard the voice of the lad where he is. Arise, lift up the lad, and hold him in thine hand; for I will make him a great nation. And God opened her eyes, and she saw a well of water; and she went, and filled the bottle with water, and gave the lad drink.

And God was with the lad; and he grew, and dwelt in the wilderness, and became an archer. And he dwelt in the wilderness of Paran: and his mother took him a wife out of the land of Egypt.

Genesis 21:1-21 (King James Version)

This is the story of the plight of Hagar, Sarah's Egyptian maid. Hagar and her son Ishmael were victims in a family crisis. Their dilemma resulted from Sarah's impulsive, impatient and even controlling nature. Interestingly, Sarah's name, before God changed it, was Sarai, which means 'heady and domineering person'. Abraham, her husband, also contributed to the dilemma because he knew what God had said to him but failed to take authority as the head of the home and insisted on following his own way. Nevertheless, when trouble erupted, God graciously intervened in the crisis and confirmed His faithfulness to His promises. God demonstrated His love, patience and care for these two families and, by extension, to us, as He turned their predicament into purpose. His divine purpose.

Background

Genesis chapters 15 and 16 give the background to the story. God had promised Abraham that he would have a son by Sarah his wife; that is, a child who would come from his own body and be his heir. However, Sarah felt that God was taking far too long to fulfil His word, and besides, she knew that her biological clock had long since ceased to tick. Consequently, it seemed to her that it would be impossible for God to make good on His promise of a child now anyway. So she decided to help Him fulfil His word to them for this son. Sarai puts another plan, her plan, into action – she gave Hagar to Abraham to be a surrogate mother for her.

So Sarai said to Abram, "See now, the LORD has restrained me from bearing children. Please, go in to my maid; perhaps I shall obtain children by her." And Abram heeded the voice of Sarai. Then Sarai, Abram's wife, took Hagar her maid, the Egyptian, and gave her to her husband Abram to be his wife, after Abram had dwelt ten years in the land of Canaan.

Genesis 16:2-3

It is interesting that Sarah had more faith in Abraham's procreative ability than her own, even though Abraham was older than she. He was eighty-six years old and she was seventy-six when she gave Hagar to him.

It is one thing for a woman to take your husband away from you, but it is quite another thing for you to purposefully give your husband to a woman so that she could have his child. Sarah had a lot of faith, but it was misplaced faith. She put her faith in man rather than God and then the trouble really started. The Scripture said that when Hagar got pregnant she became conceited and disrespectful to her employer, Sarah (Genesis 16:4). That was certainly not a wise response in this situation.

SHE PUT HER FAITH IN MAN RATHER THAN GOD AND THEN THE TROUBLE REALLY STARTED.

Of course, Sarah reacted like any other woman would. She probably said, "You have got to be mad. You've got my husband, have a child for him and now you are disrespecting me in my own house? You can't be serious!" Sarah didn't put Hagar out of her house, but the treatment she meted out to her apparently was crueler than if she had done so. The Scripture said *"Sarai dealt harshly with her"* – Genesis 16:6. Some commentators have stated that Sarah treated Hagar badly, not only with words but with blows. Actually, the same Hebrew word used for 'harsh' here is the same word used in Exodus 1:1 to describe how the Egyptian taskmasters afflicted the children of Israel. The reality was Hagar suffered some kind of abuse for her rude and unwise behavior toward Sarah. The whole affair sounded like a soap opera!

The dramas that are played out in the Old Testament can be compared to today's daytime soap operas in terms of entertainment and intrigue. In fact, by reading the Old Testament, you will be certainly entertained and educated. The Old Testament is not 'old' as in antiquated or outdated; but rather, the stories of the lives and experiences of the people are as relevant as tomorrow's news. The Old Testament books of the Bible are full of intrigue and drama: stories of betrayal, lies, arson, treason, wars, infanticide, suicide, homicide, genocide, rape, sibling rivalry, jealousy and envy, stealing, robbery, government corruption, incest, seduction, wife swapping, adultery, family squabbles, business mergers, interracial marriages, racial prejudice, bribes, gang wars, con artists, gamblers and the list goes on. The difference, however, is that in the midst of it all, you'll always find the redemptive power of God's love, His mercy and grace. You will discover how He deals with broken lives and situations and puts them back together. In these stories we find ourselves, we find hope and solutions, and we find God Himself. With these real-life accounts within our reach, why would anyone want to watch empty soap operas?

Hagar the Fugitive

Unable to put up with the harsh treatment any longer, Hagar, who by this time was well into her pregnancy, ran away. Dejected, hurt and alone, she found herself in the wilderness by the spring on the way to Shur (Genesis 16:7). Shur is just outside the eastern borders of Egypt; this suggests that Hagar was trying to get back to her homeland. Isn't that just like us when things get rough and we are in trouble? We tend to head to a place of comfort and security, that is, to familiar surroundings. The Hebrew word 'Shur' means 'wall'. Hagar was heading right into a wall.

This woman Hagar represents all of us at various times in our life experiences. We become embroiled in circumstances not always of our own making, carrying something not of our own choice, and then find ourselves with our backs against a wall – alone, depressed, hurt and afraid.

IN THESE STORIES WE FIND OURSELVES, WE FIND HOPE AND SOLUTIONS, AND WE FIND GOD HIMSELF.

The thing is that when we try to escape some situations before God accomplishes what He wants to, we head right into walls. Another thing about walls is that we put them up to protect ourselves, saying, "No one is going to take advantage of me like that again. I will never allow anyone to get close to hurt me anymore." However, those same walls that keep people out in turn imprison us.

Shur, the wall, also represents coming face to face with oneself. At Shur Hagar had to come face to face with her behavior and attitude toward Sarai. She had to face the fact that her bad attitude was responsible for her ending up in this place.

At this point, at the spring, Hagar had a profound God-encounter. The Scriptures said the Angel of the Lord found Hagar by a spring of water (Genesis 16:6-9). First, He asked her a question: *"Hagar, Sarai's maid, where have you come from, and where are you going?"* – Genesis 16: 8. God loves to ask questions. He wants us to take personal inventory of where we are emotionally, spiritually, and otherwise. In Genesis 3:9, the Lord asked Adam, *"Where are you?"* In essence, He is asking us to locate ourselves. Adam's response was not, *"I am here in the garden"* but, *"I heard Your voice in the garden, and I was afraid because I was naked; and I hid myself"* – Genesis 3:10. He answered honestly, stating that he was terrified because he messed up and was ashamed. It is not about our geographic location – God wants honesty.

Hagar answered half the question: *"I am fleeing from the presence of my mistress Sarai"* – Genesis 16: 8. She wasn't about to tell God that she was heading into a wall, which He already knew. He then told her to return to her mistress and submit herself to her. You could almost hear Hagar thinking, "Are you crazy? The woman brutalized me, treated me like dirt and You want me to go back to her!"

The Angel of the Lord continued to speak and gave Hagar promises of His faithfulness to her and her descendants, affirming and encouraging her: *"...you shall bear a son and you shall call his name Ishmael, because the Lord has heard your affliction..."* – Genesis 16: 11. It is amazing; it says He *"heard your affliction"*. I would have expected it to say, "He has seen your affliction." This tells me affliction has a voice as we will see a bit later.

When we see the Angel of the Lord in Scripture, it means it is God Himself who shows up on the scene. When He shows up, He never leaves us the way He found us. From the onset of this woman's situation, God demonstrated His love and care for her. God's tender treatment of Hagar is not unique to her but represents a component of His character and heart toward us: *"A father of the fatherless, a defender of widows, is God in His holy habitation"* – Psalm 68:5. *"The Lord watches over the strangers; He relieves the fatherless and widow"* – Psalm 146:9.

God sent Hagar back to Sarah and Abraham. Even though the atmosphere in the family would have been hostile and uncomfortable for her, it was far better than being alone in the wilderness and facing death. Her return was also for practical reasons because she was pregnant and needed the care of the family, nutrition and all that was necessary to birth this child. Remember she was carrying Abraham's seed. If she had stayed and continued on her way to Egypt, she and the baby she was carrying would have been at risk. Besides, there was unfinished business to be dealt with. God had a plan to bring her and Ishmael into a place of healing and of prosperity. God is, and cannot be anything but Himself, the One who cares for people. He shows Himself to be the God who *"sets the solitary in families; He brings out those who are bound into prosperity"* – Psalm 68:6.

God will not allow you to run away from your problems, especially if you are pregnant with His promises. You have to go back to face some things; otherwise, you and that promise could run into trouble.

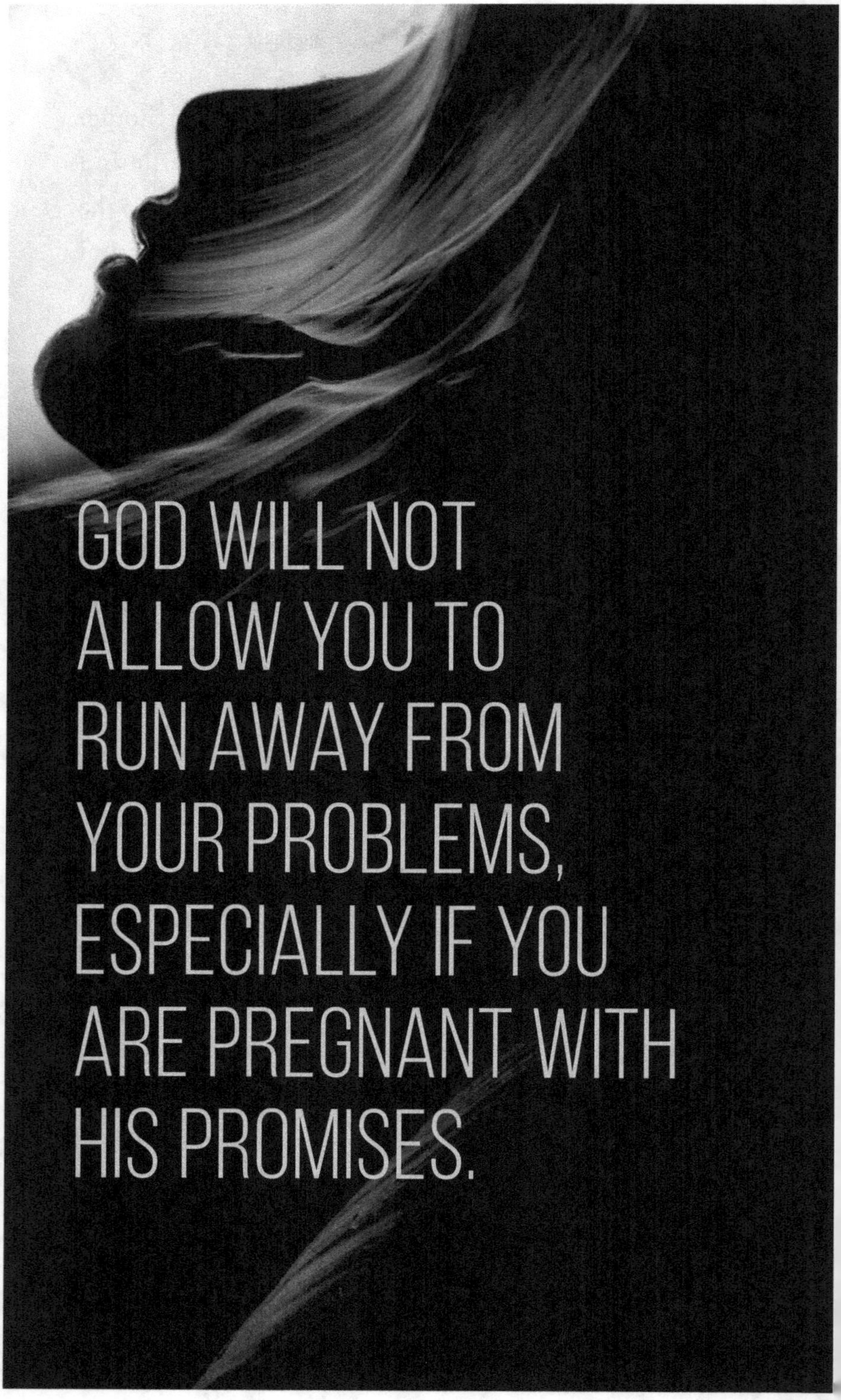

GOD WILL NOT
ALLOW YOU TO
RUN AWAY FROM
YOUR PROBLEMS,
ESPECIALLY IF YOU
ARE PREGNANT WITH
HIS PROMISES.

SCENE 1

GOD KEPT HIS PROMISE

And the Lord visited Sarah as He had said,
and the Lord did for Sarah as He had spoken.

Genesis 21:1

Had Sarah waited on God's timing, all the drama, sorrow and heartache experienced by both these families would have been avoided. Scripture teaches us that God's Word will not return unto Him unaccomplished (Isaiah 55:14). In spite of all the confusion and trauma Sarah's impetuous action caused, God still kept His promise to her and Abraham for a son. I am so thankful for God's faithfulness. You may have messed up, but thank God for His faithfulness. 1 Thessalonians 5:24 states that *"Faithful is He who calls you who will also do it."*

Sarah operated in the flesh to solve what she felt was a problem. Scripture admonishes us that we owe the flesh nothing and should not live after its dictates, for if we let the flesh rule our actions we will die; but if we, by the Spirit, put to death the deeds of the body we will live (Romans 8:12-13). Death is always the end result of the works of the flesh. Sarah's impulsive, fleshly actions became the cause of pain for all of them, especially Hagar, resulting in the birth of Ishmael and almost led to his death.

Would Ishmael Please Stand Up?

Ishmael was fourteen years old when Sarah gave birth to her promised Isaac. Ishmael was, and continued to be, the source of Hagar's grief, shame and rejection. It would be good at this point if you could identify some of your Ishmaels. Who or what is an Ishmael? Anytime you go your way and do your own thing, contrary to God's set order, an Ishmael is conceived.

Sometimes an Ishmael is conceived through no fault of your own. It could be the scar of childhood abuse – sexual, emotional, physical or psychological. It could be the pain of a broken relationship, divorce, betrayal, or the guilt and shame of a former lifestyle. We could continue to identify what an Ishmael is for each of us because we all have had, or have, them in our lives. The pain in our lives is sometimes the outcome of someone else's action or as a result of our own disobedience, willfulness and sin. Regardless of who or what is responsible, there is a "but God" for that situation.

Ishmael the Mocker

So the child (Isaac) grew and was weaned. And Abraham made a great feast on the same day that Isaac was weaned. And Sarah saw the son of Hagar the Egyptian, whom she had borne to Abraham, scoffing.

Genesis 21:8-9

Isaac had just been weaned and would have been about four years old, and Ishmael now a teenager, about seventeen years old. One day, Sarah caught him mocking her child, Isaac. When Hagar was pregnant, she despised and resented Sarah; now her son is mocking his half-brother, Isaac. Like mother like son.

The promise of a son to Abraham had been fulfilled; there were now two children in the house: Isaac, meaning 'laughter', the promised child, and Ishmael, the mocker. Laughter and mocking cannot comfortably co-exist. The word 'mock' means more than just a casual insult or jeer. In fact, the Apostle Paul called it 'persecution'. In Galatians 4:28-29, he said, *"Now we, brethren, as Isaac was, are children of promise. But, as he who was born according to the flesh then persecuted him who was born according to the Spirit, even so it is now."*

WHEN GOD BIRTHS A PROMISE IN YOUR LIFE AND IT COMES TIME FOR IT TO MANIFEST, THE ISHMAELS OF YOUR PAST WILL TRY TO DRIVE YOUR PROMISE AWAY BY PERSECUTING IT.

A weaned child is one step closer to becoming independent. When God births a promise in your life and it comes time for it to manifest, the Ishmaels of your past will try to drive your promise away by persecuting it. Ishmael might have said something like, "Ha! You, a father of nations? I was here before you and I have firstborn rights. I am the rightful owner of the inheritance."

Ishmael mocked and harassed Isaac with his words, but he mocked Sarah and Abraham with his presence. He was a painful reminder to them of their lack of faith in the promises of God. Ishmael's presence said, "If you had waited on God and trusted His word, all this would not have happened." I ask you, what is your Ishmael mocking you and saying? The good news is that you do not have to be harassed by Ishmael any more.

Enough is Enough!

Therefore she said to Abraham, "Cast out this bond-woman and her son; for the son of this bondwoman shall not be heir with my son, namely with Isaac. And the matter was very displeasing in Abraham's sight because of his son. But God said to Abraham, "Do not let it be displeasing in your sight because of the lad or because of your bondwoman.

Whatever Sarah has said to you, listen to her voice; for in Isaac your seed shall be called.

Genesis 21:10-12

If you want to see a mother go crazy, mess with her child. Sarah had had enough of Ishmael's mocking, and for his persecution of the promised child, Isaac, she ordered that Hagar and her son be driven away and expelled. Sarah knew that Ishmael was the firstborn and so had claim to the inheritance. So when she said, *"Cast out the bondwoman and her son"* she was not only saying, "Divorce Hagar, get rid of her" but also, "Disinherit Ishmael". Sarah demanded that Abraham divorce Hagar and so legally exclude Ishmael from all claim on the inheritance. God agreed because He had designed that succession be established in the line of Isaac (See Genesis 17:21).

Earlier when Hagar ran away (Genesis 16), the Lord sent her back to Sarah, but now He agreed that it was time for Ishmael to be removed. Hagar probably questioned the Lord, saying, "This makes no sense! When I ran away the first time, You sent me back and now You are agreeing that my son and I be sent away? What is going on?" Little did Hagar realize that God was working out His plan for both of them. His plans for you are for good and not for evil (Jeremiah 29:11).

God had said in Genesis 16:12 that Ishmael would be a wild man and his hand would be against every man. Ishmael's quick temper and warlike disposition, together with his taunting, were a threat to the survival of the promised child, Isaac. It was therefore indeed time for him to go. When Jesus shared the parable of the wheat and the tares, one of the lessons He taught His disciples was the importance of timing (Matthew 13:24 –30). Jesus taught His followers that when the servants suggested that they would weed out the tares in the field to separate them from the wheat, the wise owner told them not to do so because they ran the risk of uprooting the wheat as well. He understood that the time would come when the wheat would be mature enough to be separated from the tares without hurting them. The time had come to separate Ishmael from Isaac. Your Father knows that in order for your promise to come to fruition Ishmael has to be removed.

Your Ishmael will mock at your promise and, if possible, kill it, but God will jealously guard that promise on your life. He will move away from you all that threatens it; if not, these threats will fight for and corrupt your rights to receiving your inheritance. In Hagar and Ishmael's case this was the right occasion to resolve this problem. Premature action would most likely have harmed both mother and child. This is the point at which they should be separated.

Sarah had the insight to know that it was time for her to expel Ishmael because her promised Isaac was coming into maturity and would have been at risk. You, too, must recognize when your promise is on the verge of being fulfilled and that it is time more than ever to deal with your Ishmaels. When you do, God will definitely come into agreement with you. Are you ready?

FOR DISCUSSION

"Being impatient is half a mistake that leads to a full mistake and eventually ends in regret." – Anonymous

Had Sarah understood the enormous impact of her impatience, surely she would have acted differently.

1. Is there a promise that God has made to you but you feel as though it is taking much too long to be fulfilled?

2. What is your posture as you wait on His word to be fulfilled?

3. How do you think rushing ahead and doing it yourself could affect your future?

4. Find and write down scriptures that speak of waiting on God's timing.

SCENE 2

HAGAR AND ISHMAEL REJECTED

Therefore she said to Abraham, "Cast out this bondwoman and her son; for the son of this bondwoman shall not be heir with my son, namely with Isaac."

Genesis 21:10

The first time Hagar ran away she was a few months pregnant, now Ishmael was a seventeen-year-old teenager and, according to Jewish culture, a man. The source of Hagar's pain had grown and had become an increasing problem for her and those around them. She was ordered to take her problem with her and leave. It was her child; she had conceived him, and nobody wanted either of them.

It must have been a ripping and heart-wrenching experience for Abraham. He must part with the firstborn son from his loins. He was in pain more than ever. There are some things that come into our lives which resemble what we have been promised and we've been praying for for a long time. On closer examination, however, we discover that they are really impostors, born not of the Spirit of God but of the flesh and self-will.

In the midst of his pain, God lovingly reassured Abraham of His promise to him: *"Yet I will also make a nation of the son of the bondwoman, because he is your seed"* – v. 13. 'Yet' means 'nevertheless, notwithstanding'. In spite of all the mess, God says, "I will still keep My word spoken over Ishmael." Even though God will separate you from that which threatens His promises from being fulfilled in your life, He still has a purpose for your Ishmael. Isn't God good! He never wastes anything. Though all things in your life may not be good, God, who cares about you, can make them work for your good! Hallelujah!!!

The No-Name Child

Up to this time Ishmael was referred to by his name, but from the time the promised child, Isaac, came on the scene, he was called anything but Ishmael. In verse 9 he is called "the son of Hagar", in verse 10 he is referred to as "the son of this bondwoman", in verses 12, 17-18 and 20 he is "the lad" and in verses 14-16, "the boy". No one wanted to acknowledge that he,

THOUGH ALL THINGS IN YOUR LIFE MAY NOT BE GOOD, GOD, WHO CARES ABOUT YOU, CAN MAKE THEM WORK FOR YOUR GOOD!

the pain, existed. This is really rejection! They did not want to be bothered with Ishmael; they just wanted to get rid of him. Isn't it funny that there are those, especially the perpetrators, who choose to act as if our rejection and hurt do not exist? No one wants to call the abuse, rape or incest. No one wants to own up to it.

So Abraham rose early in the morning, and took bread and a skin of water; and putting it on her shoulder, he gave it and the boy to Hagar, and sent her away.

Genesis 21:14a

Abraham gave bread, a skin of water and Ishmael to Hagar and sent them away. In those days, since there were no stores around to buy food when travelling, it was customary that you take enough supplies to last until you got to the next village or encampment. At first it may appear that this was what Abraham did – that he gave Hagar enough to last them until they got to the next village. But what are a skin of water and a loaf of bread to a teenage boy and a mother in the desert? Those of us who have teenage boys know that they can "eat you out of house and home" in a short space of time.

What made Abraham's actions more appalling was that he was a very rich man. He owned a tremendous amount of livestock and real estate. Earlier we read in Genesis 21:8 that he had had a great feast for Isaac. In those days feasts would last for at least two days or even a week; therefore, Abraham was by no means short on supplies; he was full of resources. Also, this was his first child! Surely he could have done better.

Abraham's attitude toward Ishmael here is puzzling; he seems ambivalent in his reaction to his son. After all, previously in Genesis 17:18, it was Abraham who cried out to God saying, *"Oh, that Ishmael might live before You!"* And now he was abandoning him into the desert with his mother and a few supplies to a sure death. It seems that Abraham just wanted to get rid of them. It says he *"sent her away"*. The word 'sent' means 'to forget, from want of memory, to be oblivious of, to push away, and to forsake'.

While, as mentioned before, Ishmael was Abraham's first fruit from his own loins, the child still represented a dark decision born out of lack of faith in God and His promises. Abraham's actions proved that he did not want them around to remind him of their failure and his disobedience. It is funny that those who have seeded your pain, those responsible for your sorrow, often push you away. They don't want to own up to it. Rather than say, "I was wrong and I am sorry. How can I make amends?" they choose to turn their backs on you. They make you feel like you were the guilty one; like you were responsible for what happened.

FOR DISCUSSION

Life is going along fine; you are minding your business and doing what is expected of you. Without warning, someone makes a decision that involves you, without your consent or your input, which alters the trajectory of your life forever. This was the case with Hagar.

1. Hagar said, *"I am fleeing from the presence of my mistress Sarai."* – Genesis 16:8. The word 'Hagar' means 'emigrant, fugitive, flight'. Hagar admitted to God that she was on the run from Sarai. What are you running from? What person(s) or situation(s) don't you want to face?

2. Who or what is an Ishmael? Ishmaels are unwanted and often unwarranted. They are usually something from your past that stands as a painful reminder in your present. Identify who or what is (are) your Ishmael(s).

3. Sarah eventually bore her son Isaac and had enough of Hagar and her son Ishmael. *"Cast out this bond woman and her son."* – Genesis 21:10. God has designated now as the time to deal with Ishmael. Are you ready? If so, what do you think has caused you to arrive at this place of readiness?

SCENE 3

LOST IN THE WILDERNESS

*Then she departed and wandered
in the Wilderness of Beersheba.*

Genesis 21:14b

The first time Hagar ran away, she managed to make it all the way to the wilderness of Shur near her homeland Egypt. But this time she was in unfamiliar territory and wandered around in the wilderness of Beersheba. The first time she was alone, but this time she was dragging along her full-grown son. Unresolved issues in your life never really go away; they have a way of growing larger and becoming a burden. Carrying them around impedes your progress so that you cannot reach your destination and fulfil purpose.

The Power of a Name

Biblical names often forecast some characteristic or history of the person who bore the name. For example, Moses means 'drawn out' because he was drawn out of the Nile River. The name Jabez means 'pain' because his mother bore him in pain. Hagar means 'emigrant, fugitive, and wanderer'. From the outset, tied up in this woman's destiny is the tendency to run away and hide from her situations instead of facing them. Hagar was all of these things. She was an emigrant from Egypt, in Genesis 16 she became a fugitive from Sarah's abuse and now a wanderer lost in the wilderness, driven out by Sarah and Abraham. With a name like Hagar she didn't have a chance. You need to be careful what you name your children, because in giving a name you can prophesy their destiny in a negative or positive way.

God is so wise; He did not allow Hagar, Sarah or Abraham to name Hagar's son. They would have probably named him out of their shame, rejection and pain due to the circumstances under which he was conceived and the tension that ensued in their relationships. So He took the responsibility of naming the child Himself – Ishmael.

There are several interesting things to note about Hagar. She had a face-to-face encounter with God. We see that in Genesis 16:13 she asked, *"Have I also here seen Him who sees me?"* She had a promise from God for her son. She also holds a special place in the history of Scripture – she was one of the few people in the Old Testament who had a visitation by the Angel of the Lord either with respect to the foretelling of the birth of their children or their names. Even though Hagar had a lot going for her she was still lost and wandering in the wilderness with her Ishmael.

To 'wander' means to 'stagger like a drunkard, go astray'. There are many Hagars in the Body of Christ who have had some real experiences in God. They also know God has given them some powerful and specific prophetic words, yet there is an inherent tendency to wander, to roam and to be led astray. Their walk is marked by inconsistency; they keep straying from God's purposes for them and from dealing with the Ishmaels that threaten their intimacy with the Father. As a result, they have lost perspective and direction in their lives and are wandering around in spiritual and emotional wildernesses. Unhealed pain will cause you to wander around in a wilderness experience, losing all perspective of your purpose and destiny.

I feel sorry for Hagar. Don't you? She did what she was told, slept with Abraham, had his child and now she has become the victim, in pain. It is so easy to feel comfortable being the victim and cherishing the attention it gets you. It frees you from taking responsibility for your situation. However, God says that the time has come to put an end to the victim mentality.

UNHEALED PAIN WILL CAUSE YOU TO WANDER AROUND IN A WILDERNESS EXPERIENCE, LOSING ALL PERSPECTIVE OF YOUR PURPOSE AND DESTINY.

He will not allow you to continue in it because there's much to be done. The last chapter has not yet been written.

Left High and Dry, Hagar Takes Action

And the water in the skin was used up.

Genesis 21:15a

The water was finished and, needless to say, the bread was also gone. Once the water was used up, and unless they got some more soon, death would be inevitable. It is possible to live longer without food than water. The water in the skin speaks of what man can give you to help with your pain, but that help is limited. It is often of the flesh and it won't be long before it is gone.

David also recognized this when he cried out in Psalm 60:11 (KJV), *"Vain is the help of man."* When you accept help from the arm of flesh, it brings temporary relief and touches only the symptoms but does not deal with the source or root of that which threatens to bring our demise. Secular counselling and therapy have their place, but there are some issues that, when the water in that skin is used up, leave no lasting solution to the problem and the pain persists. If there is no immediate help you will eventually die – emotionally and spiritually.

The Big Cover Up

She placed the boy under one of the shrubs.

Genesis 21:15b

Hagar is now at the beginning of the end of herself. Man could do nothing for her and so she did what she knew to do. The first thing she did was to cast, as the King James Version states, her son under one of the shrubs. The word 'cast' or 'placed' comes from the Hebrew word meaning 'to send away, to hurl, and to throw'; this indicated that she pushed Ishmael away from her. The rejected becomes the rejecter. This is what usually happens; you experience rejection and in turn perpetuate the cycle of rejection by rejecting others. You reject them before they reject you.

She may have said, "I am going to reject Ishmael and deny his existence by hiding him under the leaves of the shrub." From Genesis to this day, man continues to have a love affair with leaves. First, Adam tried to cover up his sin with fig leaves, and then he tried to hide from the presence of God among the trees in the garden. Hagar endeavored to hide her pain under leaves and bushes, but we also try to hide our Ishmaels with them.

When you think of it, it is ludicrous to try to hide a seventeen-year-old young man under a little shrub. But that is how it looks when you try to cover your Ishmaels with shrubs. You use shrubs of religious activity, shrubs of accomplishments, and shrubs of involvement with this cause or that cause. "I will sing in the choir, I will be the best usher there is, or dancer, worship leader, intercessor or pastor..." Some even come to church to anesthetize the pain with 'shrubs' but do not deal with the real issues. For some, shrubs are titles at work or organizations, for others they are name brand clothing and power suits, or shrubs of academic and corporate accomplishments, and the list goes on. You keep on hiding from reality. Like Hagar, you try to reject the existence of your pain by covering it up with all types of acceptable external trappings.

Then she went and sat down across from him at a distance of about a bowshot; for she said to herself, "Let me not see the death of the boy."

Genesis 21:16a

Hagar believed death was inevitable; therefore, she could not bear to see her son die, but at the same time she didn't want to lose sight of him. So she put the distance of a bowshot between them, which, according to the Jews, was about half a mile (John Gill's Exposition of the Bible). Hagar covered up Ishmael and then distanced herself from him. That's exactly what some have done. You have said, "If I ignore it, it will go away. If I don't acknowledge it, it will die." You try to bury your issues alive; however, unresolved issues do not die.

The Scriptures said that Hagar did not want to see the death of her son. She was speaking death, but didn't God promise her earlier that Ishmael would live to be a great man? God had said, *"I will multiply your descendants exceedingly, so that they shall not be counted for multitude"* (Genesis 16:10). It is amazing how quickly you can forget the promises of God.

When pain comes, you choose to believe the lie of the enemy that accuses God of not keeping His word. Then you begin to confess death as Hagar did. You feel that it is no use; you have gone too far, He can't use you, your life is too messed up, and you have made too many wrong choices. If you keep following Hagar and her Ishmael you will see that is anything but the truth.

She lifted up her voice and wept.

Genesis 21:16b

Finally, Hagar reaches the breaking point. She opened her mouth and wept bitterly. It is the cry that reaches the ear of God, a heartfelt cry. This is what He had been waiting for all along. Psalmist David said, *"In my distress I called upon the Lord and cried out to my God; He heard my voice from His temple, and my cry came before Him, even to His ears"* – Psalm 18:6. That is what it will take for some. The Lord is awaiting a cry from you. Not necessarily a cry of tears, even though tears most likely will be involved, but a cry of desperation, a cry that says,

"Lord, man has tried to help me, I have tried to help myself, but I need You to intervene on my behalf."

And God heard the voice of the lad.

Genesis 21:17a

Now, God really gets involved! It is not that He wasn't involved all along. He certainly was, because He was all the while orchestrating circumstances to bring Hagar to this point. God was waiting to hear and to respond to an honest heartfelt cry. All it takes is a cry, and He will hear. A true father's heart hears his children's cries. Paul says, *"For you did not receive the spirit of bondage again to fear, but you received the Spirit of adoption by whom we cry out, 'Abba, Father'"* – Romans 8:15; however, while it is unfortunate, Father usually has to wait until we come to the end of ourselves where we cry out in desperation.

It was Hagar who cried, but, interestingly, the Scripture said that, *"God heard the voice of the lad"* – Genesis 21:17. Hagar had become so connected, so intimate with her pain, that when she cried it was the voice of her son Ishmael that God heard. Sometimes people can't tell the difference between you and your pain. They label you as the pain, but God knows how to make the distinction. He knows that the pain is not really you.

Ishmael has a voice. Your pain has a voice and it cries out all the time to be healed even before you do. Pain takes on an expression all of its own, and it will not be silenced. No amount of ignoring it, hiding it, covering it, singing and shouting or dancing it down will silence it. Regardless of what you do, your sin, sorrow or suffering will find a voice. It will find ways of expressing itself so that it will be heard, seen or felt. Whether in a language of self-pity, aggression, insecurity, anger, rage, lust, hostility, passivity, it will express itself. You cannot hide pain; God hears its cry. Other people hear it too but not quite like God does. He hears it with ears of compassion and mercy.

David said when he had called upon the Lord in his distress that the Lord *"bowed the heavens also, and came down"* – Psalm 18:9. When God comes on the scene it is to bring healing and restoration; it is not to cast blame or to receive excuses or explanations. In order to do this He had to take Hagar through a process which brought her face to face with that which she had rejected. God knows that you cannot conquer that which you won't confront and what is concealed cannot be healed. So, step-by-step, He took her back to face her Ishmael. It is all about coming to a place of honesty, to a place where you get rid of the pretense. Proverbs 28:13 says, *"He who covers his sins will not prosper, but whoever confesses and forsake them will have mercy."*

GOD KNOWS THAT YOU CANNOT CONQUER THAT WHICH YOU WON'T CONFRONT AND WHAT IS CONCEALED CANNOT BE HEALED.

FOR DISCUSSION

Hagar's trials and ultimate triumph provide valuable insights and solutions that would help you to be victorious in the end.

1. Hagar and her son became wanderers in the wilderness. *"Then she departed and wandered in the wilderness of Beersheba."* – Genesis 21:14b. Your Ishmael will eventually cause you to end up in the wilderness. Have you been there? Describe your wilderness experience.

2. Hagar tried to hide Ishmael. *"She placed the boy under a shrub"* – Genesis 21:15b. What 'shrubs' are you using to cover up your Ishmael?

3. *"Then she went and sat down across from him a distance... for she said to herself, 'let me not see the death of the boy.'"* – Genesis 21:16a. Are you in denial or trying to ignore the fact that there is an Ishmael(s) in your life? What do you think is at the root of your denial or desire to ignore your Ishmael(s)?

4. Hagar *"lifted her voice and wept, and God heard the voice of the lad."* – Genesis 21:16b; 17a. God hears the cry of your pain. What sound does your cry give out? What does it mean to you that God hears the cry of Ishmael?

SCENE 4

GOD'S RESTORATION PLAN: PART I

And God heard the voice of the lad. Then the angel of God called to Hagar out of heaven, and said to her, "What ails you, Hagar? (KJV expresses it as "What aileth thee, Hagar?"). Fear not, for God has heard the voice of the lad where he is."

Genesis 21:17

The God Who Hears, Responds

God had been silent all along, watching and waiting for the right moment to intervene; and now He was about to take Hagar through a process of restoration. Was God indifferent to her pain? No, it was about timing. Hagar had come to the end of herself. The same way you have to come to the end of yourself, and, when you do, He will begin the process.

And now He begins:

1. He Asked a Question. *"What aileth thee, Hagar?"* – vs. 17a

God starts the process of restoration by asking a question. We know God is famous for His rhetorical questions. In Exodus 4:2 He asked Moses, *"What is that in your hand?"* and He asked Ezekiel, *"Can these bones live?"* – Ezekiel 37:3. In the New Testament Jesus asks the lame man lying at the pool, *"Do you want to be made well?"* – John 5:6. You feel like responding, "Isn't it obvious?" But the answer to the question is not for Him but for us.

Hagar had been questioned before by the Angel of the Lord in Genesis 16:8. This time He asked, *"What aileth thee…?"* (KJV). The purpose was to bring Hagar to the point of conscious awareness of her situation. So be prepared. The first thing God will do is to ask you a question. It is to bring you to the place where you must acknowledge that there is something wrong and cause you to determine whether you truly want something done about it. When Jesus asked the lame man at the pool if he wanted to be well or whole, He was putting the responsibility on him to make a choice. Wholeness demands that we give up the victim mentality, the dependency, the blame, and the right to stay hurt. Wholeness needs your participation. Wholeness calls for responsibility to stay whole.

WHOLENESS DEMANDS THAT WE GIVE UP THE VICTIM MENTALITY, THE DEPENDENCY, THE BLAME, AND THE RIGHT TO STAY HURT.

This question is critical to the whole process. How you answer makes all the difference. What is it that you left by the side of the road? What ministry have you abandoned because someone lied on you and betrayed you? You may respond in denial, "Who, me? I don't have a problem. Can't you see how God is using me? Can't you see the anointing on my life? What could be wrong?" Denial will only prolong your wilderness experience.

What Aileth Thee? This is an interesting question. I couldn't find anywhere in Bible concordances the meaning for 'aileth' or 'ail'. So I kept on brooding over it and asking the Lord to tell me what it meant in the original language and He answered in a different way – through a dream. In the dream He gave me the name of the man (which I do not remember now) who researched it and gave its meaning. He said, 'aileth' means 'to be suffering from that which will bring you down to the grave'.

That which you try to hide, ignore and distance yourself from, if not dealt with, will eventually bring death. It will bring death to your dreams, your marriage, relationships, businesses, your ministry, and eventually your destiny. If it is unconfessed and habitual sin, I dare say, it could lead to eternal death.

Webster's English Dictionary says 'to ail' means 'to affect with pain or uneasiness in body or mind, to give pain, to trouble'. Let me add here, doctors have confirmed that many physical sicknesses have their roots in unhealed emotional pain.

God asks the question to you, "What aileth thee?" What it is that you are hiding and refusing to deal with which is going to kill you? He already knows what it is; He just wants you to acknowledge it, or as they say, "fess up". Ishmael is your child. Is it unforgiveness over some abuse, the pain of rejection and ostracism, an addiction to some secret sin, or a broken heart from a relationship gone sour? What is it? You fill in the blanks.

It is no secret that many prominent ministers of the gospel have been brought to open shame because they failed to deal with their Ishmaels in private. They hid their Ishmaels, made excuses for them, and even lied about their existence. God, because He is a loving Father, has had to discipline them publicly in order for them to deal with it and repent. This need not happen to any of us.

The beauty about surrendering your pain to God's healing process is that He does not ask questions arbitrarily. After Jesus' resurrection He appeared to His disciples at the Sea of Tiberius where they had been fishing all night without success. He asked them, *"Children, have you any food?"*– John 21:5, to which they replied in the negative. Jesus then instructed them to try again, this time casting their net on the right side. When His disciples came ashore the second time, their nets overflowing with the abundance of their catch, they found that Jesus already had a meal of fish and bread prepared and waiting for them (v. 10). It teaches us that God's provision and His solutions always accompany His questions.

GOD NOT ONLY HEARS BUT HE KNOWS EXACTLY WHERE IT HURTS AND HOW BADLY IT HURTS.

2.   He Addressed Her Fear. *"Fear not"* – v. 17b

When God comes on the scene, there is no need to fear because He is Jehovah Shalom, the God of Peace. God was saying to Hagar, "Don't worry. I have got it all under control." He is the God of comfort and the One who delivers from death. He can say "fear not" because He knows the final outcome.

3.   He Acknowledged that He was Aware of Her Situation. *"For God has heard the voice of the lad where he is."* – v. 17c

God acknowledges that He has heard her cry and knows where the lad is. Sometimes, try as you may, you could never really fully explain to someone the depths of your pain and how it hurts. God not only hears but He knows exactly where it hurts and how badly it hurts. He is touched by the feelings of your infirmities. Isn't it comforting to know how faithful our God is to us?

What is so interesting about the name 'Ishmael' is that it means 'God hears'. Remember God gave Ishmael his name in Genesis 16. He doesn't name you according to your pain like Jabez's mother did (1 Chronicles 4:9). She probably had a painful pregnancy and delivery and or Jabez's father caused her much grief. Whatever the reason, Jabez's mother named him according to her experience. She made a permanent decision on a temporary issue and her son was labelled for life with that name. It is amazing how people label us because of our pain. But thank God for the voice of pain. Jabez cried out on his own behalf and was mightily blessed (1 Chronicles 4:10).

God sees pain and sorrow in a different way than we do. He knows the power of His redemptive love to transform that pain into something beautiful. He named Ishmael 'God hears' after Himself. In doing so, God took unto Himself the stigma of the sin and rejection that this child bore, this 'illegitimate' child, a product of the relationship his mother had with a married man. Isaiah 53:4 says, *"Surely He has borne our griefs and carried our sorrows."*

God has bound Himself so intimately to you that He arranges that your pain carry His name: 'Shama' – to hear and 'el' – God (God hears). He is a Man of Sorrows and One acquainted with grief (Isaiah 53:3).

God hears and He intends to do something about your situation. Apostle John says, *"Now this is the confidence that we have in Him, that if we ask anything according to His will, He hears us. And if we know that He hears us, whatever we ask, we know that we have the petitions that we have asked of him"* – 1 John 5:14-15. It is important for you to know that if no one else hears your silent cries, God does.

FOR DISCUSSION

God always has a plan in place for your restoration, just as He did for your and my salvation before the foundations of the earth.

What Aileth Thee? – Genesis 21:17a. Go over the definition of 'aileth' in this chapter.

1. Are you ready to come clean? What is ailing you?

2. *God Addresses Your Fear* – List the things you are afraid of.

3. *God Acknowledges that He is Aware of Your Situation* – Write out scriptures of affirmation that God is with you and knows your situation.

SCENE 5

GOD'S RESTORATION PLAN: PART II

*Arise, lift up the lad and hold him with your hand, for
I will make him a great nation. Then God opened her eyes,
and she saw a well of water. And she went and filled the skin
with water, and gave the lad a drink.*

Genesis 21:17

4. It is Time to Alter Your Position. *"Arise"* – v. 18a

This is the next step in the process. 'To arise' means 'to change your posture, or position; to get up from that familiar place'. And what is familiar is that place of crying and moaning, of hopelessness and despair, regret, self-pity and condemnation. Get up from the depression in which circumstances have kept you (cf. Isaiah 60:1). yourself, and, when you do, He will begin the process.

Before you can get out of a situation, you first have to get up. We have learnt to live in ruts, to tolerate even unbearable situations, and this makes change difficult. It takes courage to change; it takes courage to arise. Nevertheless, God still says "Arise", get up, because He has empowered you to do it.

God doesn't ask you to do anything that He has not already empowered you to do. When Jesus told the man at the pool at Bethesda to arise, take up his bed and walk, it was in the obedience to the command that the power was released to accomplish the task (John 5:2-8).

There are three areas in which you need to arise:

- Get up in your attitude – *"Why are you cast down, O my soul? And why are you disquieted within me? Hope in God"* – Psalm 42:11a. The writer of the Psalm decided that it was time to have an attitude check. He realized his attitude will determine his altitude – the level to which he would arise. Change your attitude toward this situation. It is not too hard for God.

- Get up in your praise – *"For I shall yet praise Him, the help of my countenance and my God"* – Psalm 42: 11b. He made a conscious decision to praise God. If you are not praising or maintaining an attitude of praise, you most likely are complaining or allowing your mind and lips to engage in negative activity. Praise will release the presence of God in your situation to work on your behalf.

- Get up in your confession – *"I shall not die, but live, and declare the works of the Lord"*– Psalm 118:17. The Psalmist made a decision; he said, "This thing is not going to kill me." You have to determine and then confess that this thing is not going to kill you because you have an unfinished assignment and that is to "declare the works of the Lord". God is saying that it is time to make a decision to move on with your life and not let this limit you any further.

5. It is Time to Accept It. *"Lift up the lad and hold him with your hand"* – v. 18b

For Hagar to lift up Ishmael and hold him with her hand, she first had to get up and go over to him. She had to stop distancing herself from Ishmael, go over to where he was and remove him from under the shrub where she had thrown him. This meant she had to expose or uncover Ishmael. The same applies to you. You have to get up and go over to that pain and identify with it and stop making excuses for it. Take a firm hold on it and assume some measure of responsibility for it. If it was not your fault, then take the responsibility to see that it is healed. Exposure scares us. We would rather hide for appearances' sake. We feel that we can't let other people know the things we are concealing; however, God is calling for exposure. He is calling you to come out from hiding behind the masks of titles, labels, appearances, achievements etc. Disclosure must come before closure.

Our God is a Master Counselor; He took Hagar back through the same steps she used to escape Ishmael. If you are to be healed from what ails you, you have to be willing to walk through the process and revisit the place you left your Ishmael. Instead of distancing yourself from it, you have to identify with it. God will take you back to the point of childlikeness, to the point where you lost your innocence, because what we cover we cannot correct.

In 2 Kings 6:5 the man lost the axe when it fell into the water while he was chopping wood. He was worried because it was borrowed and so he went to Elisha for help, and Elisha asked to show him the place where it fell. Why? Because recovery is possible when we can identify the point of loss.

6.   He Reminds Her of His Assignment for Ishmael. *"For I will make him a great nation"* – v. 18c

God had not forgotten His promise to Ishmael. He never

GOD WILL TAKE YOU BACK TO THE POINT OF CHILDLIKENESS, TO THE POINT WHERE YOU LOST YOUR INNOCENCE, BECAUSE WHAT WE COVER WE CANNOT CORRECT.

forgets or changes His mind when He gives His word. His gifts and calling are without repentance (Romans 11:29). In spite of ostracism, rejection, and even though you may disqualify yourself because of failure, sin and shame, if you will honestly do what the Holy Spirit is telling you, you will find that God has an assignment for your pain. God reaffirms His promise to you and your Ishmael. That thing that has caused you to be in an emotional, spiritual, and mental wilderness, He has a plan for it. He said to Hagar, *"I will make him a great nation."*

There are nations in your Ishmael; it's not only about you, but nations of people are awaiting the testimony of your transformed Ishmael.

7. He Averted Her Attention from Her Situation to His Abundant Provision for Her Need. *"God opened her eyes and she saw a well of water."* – v. 19a

Webster's English Dictionary states that 'opened' means 'made plain, freed from obstruction, revealed'. God had to free Hagar's eyes from obstruction. He averted her attention from being self-absorbed to see the well of His provision. Was it that God suddenly made a well of water to appear? No, it was there all the time. Hagar could not see it because of the position she was in. That is why the first instruction God gave to her to act upon in the process of restoration was to arise, to change her posture. She had been in a position where she was so absorbed in her pain that she was unable to perceive the boundless provision God had for her.

When Hagar's eyes were opened, when her eyes were freed from obstruction, then she saw. Rather than a skin of water that man provided in the past, she saw God's abundant source awaiting her – a well of water. A never-ending supply! God likes meeting people at the well. The woman in John 4 had six Ishmaels, so to speak, but she met Jesus – the Source of Living Water – at the well and was eternally satisfied.

Sorrow, heartache and sin will blind you to the fullness of God's provision for your life. You cannot receive what the Father has for you if you are in a position of denial and refuse to confront Ishmael; however, the Lord will open your eyes to see the well as you stay true to the process. But then you must also draw deep from that well, the well of His provision and presence that is waiting to satiate your entire being.

8. It is Time to Apply His Provision. *"And she went and filled the skin with water, and gave the lad a drink."* – v. 19b

God made the provision available, but the next step was Hagar's responsibility. She had to draw from the well herself. The same skin that Abraham gave her earlier with the water that ran out is the one she used to dip from the well. This time, the water she and her son drank was from a limitless supply. There are some things

GOD DOES NOT WASTE ANYTHING. HE WILL GATHER UP THE FRAGMENTS OF YOUR LIFE AND PUT THEM TO GOOD USE.

God will not do for you. Isaiah 12:3 says, *"Therefore with joy you will draw water from the wells of salvation."* There is an abundant provision in God, in His Word, and in His presence for you to be restored, but you have to position yourself to receive it and then apply it. A sip once in a while will not do. Jesus said, *"But whoever drinks of the water that I shall give him will never thirst. But the water that I shall give him will become in him a fountain of water springing up into everlasting life"* – John 4:14. He promises life-giving water to revive and to sustain us and those things in our lives that are on the verge of death.

The account of this family drama concludes with, *"So God was with the lad; and he grew and dwelt in the wilderness, and became an archer..."* – Genesis 21:20-21. The restoration process was complete; God delivered her and her son from death to live productive lives. Ishmael not only lived but he "grew". The word 'grew' means 'he became great and important; he increased and did great and excellent things', just as God had promised. He did not renege on His promises to Hagar and Abraham about their son Ishmael; He remained faithful to His word (See Genesis 16:10; 17:20).

The outcome is the same for those who would stay with Him in the process. God does not waste anything. He will gather up the fragments of your life and put them to good use.

The story ends but Ishmael does not.

FOR DISCUSSION

Your restoration requires your participation as well.

1. *God Challenges You to Arise* – Are you ready to shift your position? What do you need to do in order to make that shift?

2. *Accept Your Ishmael* – No more running or denial. Are you willing to face your Ishmael(s), without shame or blame? What would you need to do in order to accept your Ishmael(s)?

3. *Realize Your Ishmael Has an Assignment* – Write out a declaration that states that God is going to turn this pain, hurt and rejection around for His glory.

4. How do you think this experience could be used to help others?

5. *God's Abundant Provision is Available* – Identify the ways that God has provided for you and your Ishmael.

6. *Apply God's Provision* – Identify practical ways in which you could apply God's provision.

EPILOGUE

ISHMAEL CONVERTED

Genesis 37:23-28 relates the account of Joseph and his brothers. His brothers hated and despised him because of his dreams and because he was favored by their father, Jacob. (The story is well worth reading again). So intense were their hatred and rejection of Joseph that they plotted to kill him and proceeded with a plan to do just that. Reuben, one of the brothers, bargained with them to just put him in a pit, in hopes that when they left he would rescue Joseph. They agreed, cast him into a pit and left him there to die. Judah, another brother, however, convinced them to sell Joseph to a band of merchants passing by on their way to Egypt. They conceded, sold Joseph into slavery in Egypt and the rest is history.

Because of the hand of God on Joseph's life, he experienced great favor and rose to national prominence in Egypt. When the famine broke out in Canaan, Joseph had his whole family relocated to Egypt where God prospered them and made them into a great nation. He became, for his family, the grand deliverer from the famine in Canaan. They went down to Egypt as a contingent of seventy people and 450 years later they emerged a nation of millions. Well, what does that have to do with Ishmael?

This band of merchants that bought and sold Joseph was Ishmaelites. Let's do a little family history. Isaac was the father of Jacob who was the father of Joseph by his wife Rachael. Therefore, Joseph was the grandchild of Isaac. Ishmael, Isaac's half-brother, is therefore Joseph's great uncle. Follow this now. Ishmael, the rejected son of Hagar and Abraham, through his descendants, became the instrument God used to save Joseph, his great nephew, from a sure death. Through this act of selling Joseph to the Egyptians, God worked out His amazing plan for Joseph and the people of Israel! God is awesome! Had Ishmael died in the wilderness, as his mother expected, it would have been the end of his posterity. But God had a purpose for him.

Remember Peter, the disciple that swore that he would never deny the Lord? Jesus knew exactly what would happen. That is why He told him, *"...Indeed, Satan has asked for you, that he may sift you as wheat. But I have prayed for you, that your faith should not fail; and when you have returned to Me, strengthen your brethren"* – Luke 22:31-32. The King James Version says, *"...when thou art converted strengthen your brethren."* Jesus knew that Peter was going to fail, but He also knew that Peter was going to turn back and be restored. He was telling him ahead of time that when he is restored from his test remember to use his experience to establish and encourage those he would encounter who would be just like he was. This is just what Ishmael accomplished through his descendants. He was converted and he helped establish and strengthen his brother Joseph.

You may have been despised, rejected and left for dead emotionally and otherwise, but let Ishmael's story encourage you. There is something valuable and meaningful that God will use you to do to bless this generation.

Through this experience the Lord teaches us how our personal Ishmaels (an injustice done to us or what we perceive as our mistake) are linked to our predestined purpose and ultimately His purpose. Partnering with God to heal our pain is not only for us and our purpose but it can have significant impact on the destinies of our children and their children, for generations to come.

THERE IS SOMETHING VALUABLE AND MEANINGFUL THAT GOD WILL USE YOU TO DO TO BLESS THIS GENERATION.

The Price is Paid

The Ishmaelite merchants paid Joseph's brothers twenty shekels of silver for him (Genesis 37:28). Silver in Old Testament times represented the price of redemption. Ishmael knew what it was to be ostracized and rejected by his stepmother, Sarah, his father, Abraham, and left to die by his own desperate mother, Hagar. But he was 'converted' and, through his descendants, he became the source of redemption for a now rejected brother. This brother, Joseph, was the grandchild of the family from which he himself had been initially cast out.

The spirit of rejection was prevalent in this family. Ishmael's half-brother, Isaac, had twins, Jacob and Esau, but it was very apparent that Isaac loved Esau more. As a result, Jacob felt unloved and rejected. Now as a father, he publicly favored Joseph over his other sons which led to this whole predicament. But God was in all of it, working it out for good.

You need to know that there is redemption in your pain. Someone who is left in a pit to die is waiting for your transformation to bring their redemption. You may have to go back to help some of the very people who have hurt and crushed you, and who threw you out with hardly any concern for whether you lived or died. You may have to deliver them from some pits, but you will have earned the right to do so because you stayed true to the process and paid the price. Ishmael had earned that right and paid the price to deliver a rejected brother. Life is funny; what goes around does come around. This time, however, your Ishmael will not mock but will show forgiveness, mercy and compassion.

Silver also signifies something precious. Now you can go back with the precious gift of the love of God to those who once abandoned you to deliver them out of a pit of pain and or sin. You will treat them with the courtesy they did not afford you. You can do that only when you are converted, only when you have been healed, made whole and transformed.

Ishmael, through his descendants, did grow and become great; he did a great thing, an excellent thing – he delivered the deliverer. Everyone talks of Joseph; however, we also need to remember it was the Ishmaelites who were instrumental in him being positioned in the right place. Joseph eventually brought his family to Egypt, delivering them from the dreadful famine in the land of Canaan and that started a new era in the history of the Israelites (Genesis 46:1-3).

"What aileth thee?" God asks. He wants you to know that the cries of your Ishmael have come up to Him. He wants to heal the Ishmaels in your life, forgive sin and redeem them, and use your transformed sorrow and suffering to bring redemption to someone else. Your Ishmael has redemptive value.

In 1 Kings 18 and 19, we have the story of Elijah and his encounter with the prophets of Baal and Jezebel. After Elijah displayed the power of God and destroyed the prophets of Baal and their high places, Jezebel confronted him and threatened to kill him. Elijah, the mighty man of God, literally ran from this woman. Refusing to face his tormentor, he forfeited the completion of his purpose to Jehu. During Jehu's reign, Jezebel and her children were killed, thus he completed the task which Elijah had abandoned (cf. 1 Kings 19:15-17; 2 Kings 9:6-10). Elijah could not go any further because he refused to face up to that which threatened his life and his destiny. If you decide not to face the Ishmaels in your life, and are determined on running from them, God will eventually release you to do so, but you would have aborted the fulfilment of your destiny.

His question today to you is What Aileth Thee? What is it that you have been carrying for so long that has developed from a baby to a full-grown adult? What is that thing which will kill you if you try to continue avoiding it like Hagar did? It will certainly kill off the purposes of God for you.

Another Price Has Been Paid

Over 2000 years ago Jesus Christ, the Son of God, came to earth to accomplish His Father's will. While on earth He was betrayed by his disciple Judas for 30 pieces of silver and denied by His disciple Peter. He was mocked, rejected, spat upon and humiliated by the religious leaders and his detractors, and then was hung on a cross to die, but not before they had stripped Him of His clothes and brutally beaten Him beyond recognition. Why? Jesus came to give His life in payment for the sin of the whole world – a ransom for your sin and mine. He took on Himself the judgment that was ours, the judgment for your sin. When He hung there on the cross moments before He died, He cried out, *"It is finished",* meaning the price has been paid in full, once and for all, for our redemption – your redemption (see John 19:30).

Ishmael was a type and shadow of Christ; he was rejected and abandoned and left to die in the wilderness by his mother, Hagar. But when God restored him he went on to help deliver his 'brother' in the person of Joseph. Jesus Christ is a fulfillment of the Old Testament picture of Ishmael. He came to seek and to save that which was lost (Luke 19:10). He came to liberate us from the misery and penalty of our sins (Mark 10:45). If you would like to, you can receive Jesus Christ as your Savior, Deliverer and Lord, and you can have the peace that your sins are forgiven and assurance that you have eternal life with Him in heaven. *"God so loved the world that He gave His only begotten Son that whosoever believes on Him should not perish but have everlasting life"* – John 3:16.

JESUS CAME TO GIVE HIS LIFE IN PAYMENT FOR THE SIN OF THE WHOLE WORLD – A RANSOM FOR YOUR SIN AND MINE.

FOR DISCUSSION

The testimony of your Ishmael will live on long after you are gone.

1. Write a declaration that God will indeed use your Ishmaels as a blessing (and not a curse) to your future generations.

2. In your quiet time with the Lord, what are some of the ways you sense that God will use your Ishmael in the future?

MY TESTIMONY

I, too, had my Ishmaels; I suffered verbal and emotional abuse and a tremendous amount of rejection. I carried an immense amount of anger, bitterness, unforgiveness and self-hatred. I hid it away very nicely, I thought, but the day came when God had me come face to face with my Ishmaels. I chose not to bury them alive anymore. The process was painful at times, but thank God for His relentless love. He did not allow me to continue ailing and neither will He allow you if you yield to Him. It is usually not a onetime event. With some things God takes His time with us because He knows how sensitive and painful they are.

It is amazing, if our doctor diagnosed us with a disease or medical problem from which we would die unless we got surgery or some type of immediate medical treatment, not many of us would hesitate or take the chance and play around with it. If we can entrust our physical lives to fallible doctors and surgeons and follow their recommendations to cure our ailments, why then can't we submit our whole lives to an infallible and loving God? He is a God who knows us and cares deeply about us individually. He wants to deal with our Ishmaels so that we do not continue to ail and eventually die. He desires that we live the abundant life in His presence, fulfilling His appointed purpose for us.

So I urge anyone reading who knows that Ishmaels are haunting you, to seek out a solid Biblical Christian counselor. Find someone who is led by the Spirit to help walk you through the healing process. I did. Mind you, there were times the Holy Spirit simply walked me through the process Himself. Whatever you do, do not continue to live in secret pain.

"What aileth thee?" Ail no longer. God has much ahead for you to accomplish. You were created for greatness!

If you'd like to find out more about my story with my Ishmaels, you can find it documented in my book ***Soul Survivor:*** *Moving from Trauma to Triumph*, available on Amazon.

Linda P. Jones (Rev.)

MY BOOKS

Download the ebook or order the paperback at Amazon.com. Paperback also available at Barbados bookstores.

Calling All Deborahs
Calling All Deborahs Workbook
Soul Survivor
21-Day Devotional for Soul Survivors
Decrees for Soul Survivor
Out of the Ashes
The Peace of God
The Radical Jesus
Exposing the Spirit of Deception
For This Child I Prayed

ABOUT THE AUTHOR

Reverend Linda Jones is an ordained minister, an expository Bible teacher and sought-after speaker. She has hosted several seminars, workshops, conferences and productions in her nation. She also pastored a ministry for several years but is now an itinerant minister. Rev. Jones is the founder of Linda P. Jones Ministries, Soul Survivor (a charitable organization for the needy), Women of Worth Ministries, and Walking on Water Teaching & Equipping Centre, also called WOWTEC e-Academy.

WOWTEC e-Academy is an online school providing sound biblical, relevant teachings that are applicable for the growth and development of believers as they walk in the purposes of God. Rev. Jones is very personable in her teaching style; her teachings are profound and yet easy to understand. Overall, she does not compromise the truth of God's Word.

She is also a radio show host and has a bi-monthly radio program, Words of Wisdom, 'bringing practical godly wisdom for everyday living'. Linda's personal mission statement is Luke 4:18-19, which is the primary thrust for the ministries she has founded. She is passionate to see individuals, especially those in the Body of Christ, healed in every dimension of their lives (spirit, soul and body), and be adequately equipped through the Word, and with the skills necessary to fulfill their destiny call, expand the kingdom of God in the earth and glorify Jesus Christ.

Linda is a prolific writer and her writings are geared to bring healing and empowerment to families, the Body of Christ and nations.

Rev. Jones holds a Bachelor of Theology from Christian International, Santa Rosa Beach, Florida, and a Master of Practical Theology from Master's International University of Divinity, Evansville, Indiana, and is pursuing her doctorate in Practical Theology. Linda is the committed wife of Oliver for over 30 years and they are the parents of one daughter.

CONTACT INFORMATION

To schedule speaking engagements, seminars and workshops, you may contact Linda P. Jones by:

Email

info@lindapjones.org

Website

www.lindapjones.org

Facebook

@pastorlindapjones

Instagram

@lpjministries

LinkedIn

linda-p-jones-ministries

Walking on Water Teaching & Equipping Centre
WOWTEC e-Academy Mentorship Program

www.wowteceacademy.com